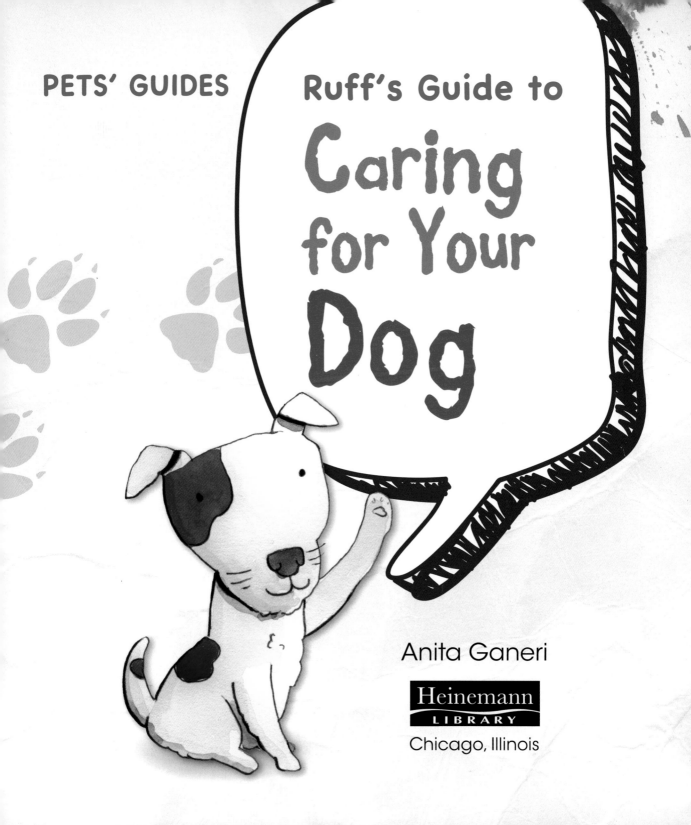

PETS' GUIDES

Ruff's Guide to
Caring
for Your
Dog

Anita Ganeri

Heinemann
LIBRARY

Chicago, Illinois

To contact Capstone Global Library please phone 800-747-4992, or visit our website www.capstonepub.com

Edited by Daniel Nunn, Rebecca Rissman, and Sian Smith
Designed by Cynthia Della-Rovere
Original illustrations © Capstone Global Library Ltd 2013
Illustrated by Rick Peterson
Picture research by Tracy Cummins
Production by Victoria Fitzgerald
Originated by Capstone Global Library Ltd
Printed in China

17 16 15 14 13 12
10 9 8 7 6 5 4 3 2 1

Library of Congress Cataloging-in-Publication Data
Ganeri, Anita, 1961-

Ruff's guide to caring for your dog / Anita Ganeri.—1st ed.
    p. cm.—(Pets' guides)
Includes bibliographical references and index.
ISBN 978-1-4329-7131-1 (hb)—ISBN 978-1-4329-7138-0 (pb) 1. Dogs—Juvenile literature. I. Title.
SF427.G346 2013
636.7—dc23   2012017279

Acknowledgments

The author and publisher are grateful to the following for permission to reproduce copyright material: Alamy p. 27 (© blickwinkel); Capstone Library p. 7 (Karon Dubke); Corbis p. 25 (© Larry Williams Associates); Getty Images pp. 9 (Thinkstock Images), 13 (Meg Takamura), 17 left (Steve Lyne), 21 (John Howard); iStockphoto p. 5 (© kristian sekulic); Photoshot p. 23 (© BSIP); Shutterstock pp. 11 (© Cheryl E. Davis), 15 (© Will Hughes), 17 right (© Alis Photo), 19 (© lifeandlove).

Cover photograph of a Jack Russell terrier reproduced with permission of Corbis (© Mike Watson/moodboard). Design elements reproduced with permission of Shutterstock (© Picsfive) and Shutterstock (© R-studio).

We would like to thank Caroline Kisko, Communications Director at the Kennel Club, for her invaluable help in the preparation of this book.

Every effort has been made to contact copyright holders of any material reproduced in this book. Any omissions will be rectified in subsequent printings if notice is given to the publisher.

Contents

Some words are shown in bold, **like this**. You can find out what they mean by looking in the glossary.

Do You Want a Pet Dog?

Hi! I'm Ruff the dog, and this book is all about dogs like me. Did you know that dogs make wonderful pets? We're fun to take for walks, and we're great company. In return, you need to look after us properly for the whole of our lives.

Being a good dog owner means making sure that I'm always cared for. I need a safe place to live, food, water, and plenty of exercise. Then I'll quickly become your best friend.

Choosing Your Dog

Dogs come in many different sizes, colors, and **breeds**. The best places to get your new pet are from an animal shelter or a good **dog breeder**. When buying a puppy, it is a good idea to watch it with its mother and see how it behaves.

Do you want a dog or a puppy? Puppies are lots of fun, but you have to train them and spend lots of time with them. It isn't fair to get a puppy otherwise. You might want to pick an older dog like me instead.

A Healthy Dog

Make sure that the dog you choose is lively and healthy, like me. Look at my shiny coat and clear, bright eyes. My nose is cold and wet. That's another sign that I am healthy.

Some dogs are very playful. Other dogs are quiet and gentle. Think about your family when you choose a dog. A shy dog might not like living in a noisy, busy house.

Getting Ready

Before you bring me home, get a few things ready. You need dog food, bowls for food and water, a brush, some toys, and a collar and **tag**. The tag should have your family's name and address on it in case I get lost. You can ask your vet about fitting a **microchip**.

I also need a cozy bed to sleep in with a
blanket or soft padding. Plastic, chew-proof
beds are best, especially for puppies. Put my
bed somewhere warm and quiet where I
won't be disturbed if I need a rest.

Welcome Home

My new home will feel strange at first, but I'll quickly settle in. When I arrive, show me where my bed is and leave me for a while to get used to it. Keep me in one room to begin with, so that I don't get scared. Then let me explore more of the house.

I should get along with other pets, once I get to know them. Many dogs live happily with other dogs and cats. Introduce me to them gently and don't leave us alone together at first. After a while, we should become friends.

Feeding Time

Woof! Woof! It's dinner time and I'm hungry. I need food and water every day to keep me fit and healthy. You can feed me dry or wet dog food. Dry food is better for my teeth. You can buy this from the pet shop or supermarket.

Ruff's Top Meal-Time Tips

 Adult dogs like me need two meals a day. Puppies need three to four smaller meals.

 Some human foods, such as chocolate, raisins, and onions, are poisonous to dogs.

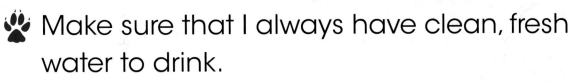 Make sure that I always have clean, fresh water to drink.

Don't feed me too many treats. They can make me overweight and unhealthy.

Sometimes give me a chewy bone to help clean my teeth.

15

Exercise

Dogs like me are energetic animals and like lots of exercise. I need to go for a walk or run twice a day. Otherwise, I'll get bored and unfit. Puppies can't go for walks until they have had their first **vaccinations** to stop them from catching diseases.

Be careful not to touch a dog's mess with your hands, and always wash your hands after picking it up.

Keep me on my leash until it is safe to let me off. Make sure that you clear up any dog mess if I go to the bathroom. Use a bag to pick up the mess and put it in the trash.

Training

Like all dogs, I need to be trained. You can train me at home or take me to a training class. Teach me to come when you call my name and to sit when you tell me to. Never shout at or hit your dog. It will make it nervous and scared.

Puppies need to be **toilet trained**. They have to learn to go to the bathroom outside. Put your puppy outside every hour and every time it wakes up or after a meal. It will soon learn that going outside means going to the bathroom.

Play Time

I love to play! My favorite game is fetching a ball. You can buy dog toys from a pet shop, but make sure that they are not too small. I especially like toys that I can chew. If I crouch down low on my front legs, it means that I'm ready to play.

I also like being stroked and patted, especially around my ears and on my chest. If I'm happy, I'll wag my tail. But if I growl or grumble, I want to be left alone. Never bother me while I'm having my dinner or having a nap in my bed.

Coat Care

Keep my coat in top condition by **grooming** me every day. This keeps my coat clean and shiny and gets rid of any old hairs. You can buy special grooming brushes from a pet shop. If I have long hair, you might need to get it **clipped**.

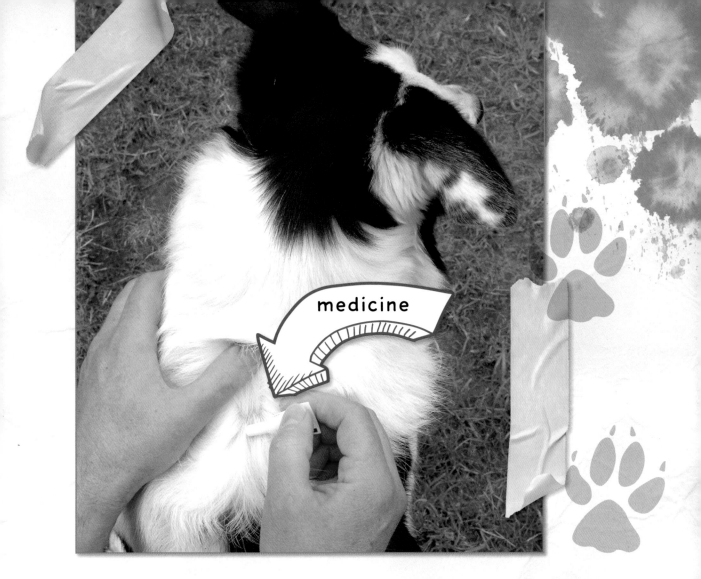

medicine

You need to check my coat regularly in case
I have **fleas**. Look for dark specks on my skin.
Then treat me with medicine from the vet.
You also need to give me medicine to help
get rid of **worms**.

Visit to the Vet

As soon as I come to live with you, take me to the vet for a checkup. Then, take me once a year for **vaccinations** to keep me healthy. Please also take me to the vet if I stop eating my food or don't seem well.

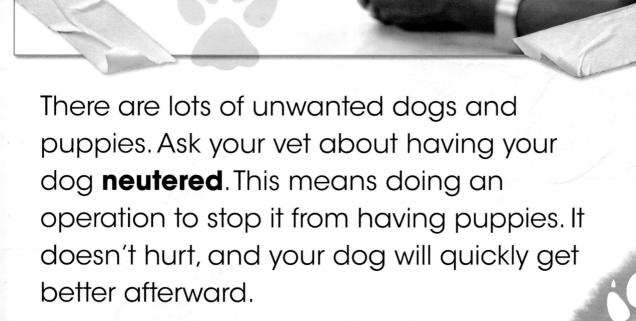

There are lots of unwanted dogs and puppies. Ask your vet about having your dog **neutered**. This means doing an operation to stop it from having puppies. It doesn't hurt, and your dog will quickly get better afterward.

Happy Vacation

If you go on vacation, you might be able to take me with you. Don't forget to pack my bed, bowls, leash, and toys. If you are driving a long way in the car, keep stopping to let me have a drink and go to the bathroom.

If you can't take me with you, please don't just leave me at home alone. Ask a friend or neighbor to stay with me or take me to their home. Otherwise, you could put me in a **boarding kennel**. It is like a hotel for dogs.

Dog Facts

 Pet dogs are all related to wolves. Wolves were probably first kept as pets about 15,000 years ago.

 There are more than 400 **breeds** of pet dogs, from tiny Chihuahuas to enormous Saint Bernards.

 Dogs have an amazing sense of smell. They can smell about a million times better than humans.

 Dogs can be trained to help people who are blind or deaf. Rescue dogs help to find people after disasters, such as earthquakes.

Helpful Tips

 If you have more than one dog, make sure that each has its own bed, toys, and food and water bowls to stop them from fighting.

 Your dog must always have a safe, quiet place where it can hide away if it feels scared or tired.

 Don't leave a dog on its own for too long. Dogs like company, or they will get bored and lonely.

 Don't leave a dog in a car on a warm day, even with a window open. It can quickly get too hot and may die.

Glossary

boarding kennel a place where you can leave your dog when you go on vacation

breeds different types of dogs or other animals

clipped when a dog's coat is cut so that it is short and tidy

dog breeder a person who has puppies or dogs looking for new homes

fleas tiny insects that can live on a dog

grooming brushing or cleaning your dog's coat

microchip a tiny chip that is put under a dog's skin. It has a special number that can be read by a scanner if the dog gets lost.

neutered when a dog has an operation so that it cannot have puppies

tag a metal circle that attaches to a dog's collar

toilet trained when a dog is taught to go to the bathroom outside

vaccinations medicines given through a needle by a vet to stop dogs from catching diseases

worms worms that grow inside your dog and can make it sick

Find Out More

Books

Bailey, Gwen, *Training Your Superpuppy*. New York: DK Publishing, 2011.

Gagne, Tammy. *Speaking Dog: Understanding Why Your Hound Howls and Other Tips on Speaking Dog*. Mankato, Minn.: Capstone, 2012.

Royston, Angela. *Dog* (Life Cycle of a...). Chicago: Heinemann, 2010.

Internet Sites

Facthound offers a safe, fun way to find Internet sites related to this book. All of the sites on Facthound have been researched by our staff.

Here's all you do: Visit www.facthound.com
Type in this code: 9781432971311

Index